YELLOWST

MILD WINTERS have CONTRIBUTED TO HUGE PINE BEETLE outbreaks
IN YELLOW-STONE PARK.
SIZE OF A RICE GRAIN

YELLOWSTONE

lake IS THE LARGEST FRESHWATER LAKE ABOVE 7000 feet IN NORTH AMERICA.

2

3

the 1ST FULL time NATURALIST in YELLOW-STONE PARK WAS Herma Albertson Baggley.

'WHAT A DRAB PLACE THE WORLD WOULD BE WERE IT NOT... BEAUTIFIED BY PLANT life'

4

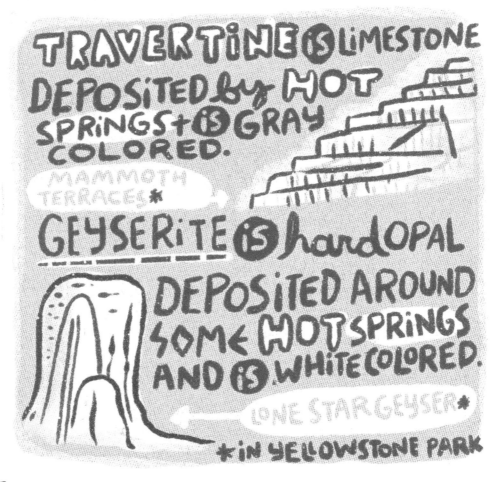

TRAVERTINE IS LIMESTONE DEPOSITED by HOT SPRINGS + IS GRAY COLORED.

MAMMOTH TERRACES *

GEYSERITE IS hard OPAL DEPOSITED AROUND SOME HOTSPRINGS AND IS WHITE COLORED.

LONE STAR GEYSER *

* IN YELLOWSTONE PARK

5

THE **YELLOWSTONE** PARK, supervolcano
HAS A **MAGMA** CHAMBER
big ENOUGH to FiLL the
GRAND CANYON **11 TIMES**.

MAGMA **CHAMBERS**

THERE ARE 3 CEMETERIES IN YELLOWTONE PARK.

FORT YELLOWSTONE | KITE HILL | TINKER'S HILL

7

the SCREW TRACTOR

was the FIRST MECHANIZED WINTER VEHICLE in YELLOWSTONE PARK.

RAISED SPIRALS PULL THE TRACTOR THROUGH SNOW.

8

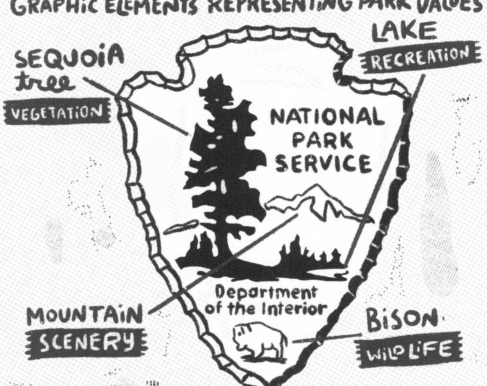

OFFICIAL NATIONAL PARK BADGE

GRAPHIC ELEMENTS REPRESENTING PARK VALUES

LAKE
RECREATION

SEQUOIA
tree
VEGETATION

NATIONAL
PARK
SERVICE

MOUNTAIN
SCENERY

Department
of the Interior

BISON
WILD LIFE

9

MAMMOTH hot SPRINGS IN YELLOWSTONE PARK HAS WISPY STRANDS OF BACTERIUM that RESEMBLE FETTUCCINI PASTA.

KNOWN AS sulfuri, scientists SEARCH FOR this 'FINGER-PRINT OF LIFE' ON OTHER PLANETS FOR PROOF OF MICRO ALIEN LIFE.

HMM

10

GEYSERS

ARE HOT springs in WHICH water BOILS + sends COLUMNS OF STEAM + WATER INTO the AIR. YELLOW-STONE HAS ABOUT 500.

11

Yellowstone SAND VERBENA IS A PLANT UNIQUE to YELLOWSTONE NATIONAL PARK. the PLANT IS so RARE THAT those WHO KNOW its WHEREABOUTS ARE SWORN to SECRECY.

12

SUPERVOLCANO

IS A 2005 DISASTER MOVIE BASED ON A FICTIONAL yellowSTONE PARK ERUPTION.

TAGLINE: IT'S UNDER YELLOW-STONE + IT'S OVERDUE.

6.7/10 IMDB

70% TOMATO-METER

14

IN 1987 A rare HIGH ALTITUDE TORNADO FLATTENED WIDE swaths OF TREES in YELLOW-STONE PARK. THE 200+ MPH WINDS ALSO RIPPED BARK OFF TRUNKS.

15

there ARE 3 U.S. NAVY SHIPS NAMED after YELLOWSTONE.

1. 1918-1919
2. 1946-1974
3. 1977 — PRESENT

16

OLD FAITHFUL is A yellowstone PARK INSPIRED -1949- PINBALL GAME.

ONLY 89 MADE!

'you can count on it!'

17

WILLIAM HENRY JACKSON

HIS survey PHOTOS HELPED CONVINCE CONGRESS TO ESTABLISH YELLOWSTONE PARK in 1872. COINCIDENTALLY his UNCLE was THE PROGENITOR OF AMERICA'S symbol UNCLE SAM.

19

SEPTEMBER 2018, YELLOW-STONE PARK'S EAR spring GEYSER HAD its STRONGEST eruption IN 60 YEARS. SOME of THE FOREIGN OBJECTS SPEWED OUT were:

COMBS

1950s FLASH BULBS

WISHING COINS

BEAR WARNING SIGNS

CONCRETE BLOCK

1930s BABY PACIFIER

1960s BEER CANS

Yellowstone Park is also known as WONDERland and is promoted as the LAND OF CURIOSITIES.

21

1988 YELLOWSTONE PARK FIRES

36% OF THE PARK burned

51 FIRES — 42 FROM LIGHTNING — 9 FROM PEOPLE

FATALITIES: 2 HUMANS

249 ELK — 9 DEER — 2 MOOSE

COST: $120 MILLION

ABOUT **3000** iTEMS ARE turned iNTO YELLOWSTONE PARK's lost + FOUND **EACH** **YEAR**. 1 OF the MOST REPORTED iTEMS LOST ARE HATS.

ELK thistle WAS RENAMED EVERT'S thistle AFTER TRUMAN EVERTS ATE the PLANT WHILE lost IN yellowstone PARK FOR 36 DAYS.

24

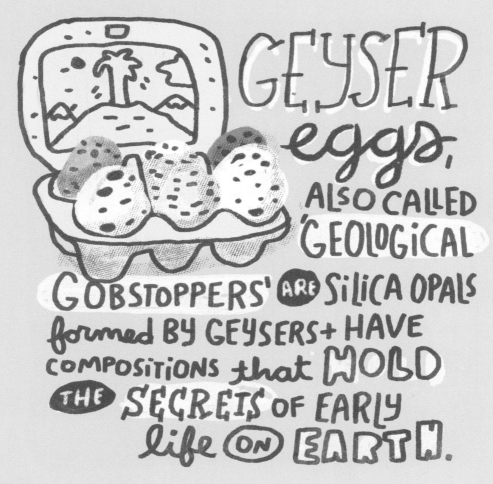

GEYSER eggs, ALSO CALLED 'GEOLOGICAL GOBSTOPPERS' ARE SILICA OPALS formed BY GEYSERS + HAVE COMPOSITIONS that HOLD THE SECRETS OF EARLY life ON EARTH.

25

26

A 2019 STUDY REVEALED that the INTENSE GRAZING HABITS + MOVEMENTS OF BISON improve YELLOWSTONE PARK'S VEGETATION. THIS INCLUDES: HIGHER NUTRITIONAL VALUE FOR PLANTS, LONGER LIVES FOR PLANTS + GREENER PLANTS.

27

BEFORE the ACTIVITY WAS BANNED, YELLOWSTONE PARK'S VISITORS COULD CATCH A TROUT IN YELLOWSTONE lake + cook it WITHIN the LAKE'S SUBMERGED HOT SPRING WITH the FISH STILL ON THE HOOK.

SO CALLED *tomato* SOUP POOLS IN YELLOWSTONE PARK HAVE *similar* ACIDITY, TEMPERATURES + COLORS AS *their* NAMESAKE.

29

YELLOWSTONE PARK is 3 · IN MONTANA

96 - IN - Wyoming

1 · -IN- iDAHO

WY

30

YELLOWSTONE PARK

is 2.2 million acres

AND IS THE 2ND largest NATIONAL PARK IN THE lower 48.

THE first PUBLISHED ACCOUNT of THE YELLOW-STONE AREA was FROM A SERIES LETTERS A FUR TRAPPER WROTE TO HIS BROTHER.

THERE ARE

3 types OF GLACIAL

DEPOSITS IN YELLOWSTONE PARK

MORAINS: LOW ROCKY HILLS FROM MELTING GLACIERS.

KETTLE POND: GLACIAL POND WATER.

ERRATICS: BOULDERS LEFT BY GLACIERS.

34

YELLOWSTONE LINGO

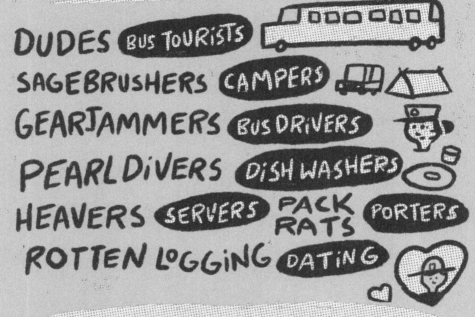

DUDES (BUS TOURISTS)

SAGEBRUSHERS (CAMPERS)

GEARJAMMERS (BUS DRIVERS)

PEARL DIVERS (DISH WASHERS)

HEAVERS (SERVERS) PACK RATS (PORTERS)

ROTTEN LOGGING (DATING)

FROM the 1929 'SONGS OF YELLOWSTONE PARK' BOOKLET.

born + RAISED IN YELLOWSTONE PARK, JANE MARGUE-RITE lindsley WAS ITS 1ST PERMANENT FEMALE PARK RANGER.

- SHE DESIGNED THE 1ST FEMALE RANGER UNIFORM FOR THE PARK
- EARNED A MASTERS IN BACTERIOLOGY
- NICKNAMED 'GEYSER PEG'

36

LiBERTY CAP iS a 37 FOOT tall DORMANT hot SPRiNG in MAMMOTH, YELLOWSTONE PARK.
LiBERTY CAP iS NAMED FOR iTS RESEMBLANCE to FRENCH REVOLUTiONARY HATS.

IN 2019 YELLOWSTONE PARK'S MOUNT HOMES. FIRE LOOKOUT BURNED DOWN FROM A LIGHTNING STRIKE. there ARE NO PLANS to REBUILD THE 1931 HISTORICAL STRUCTURE.

38

in 2017 A MAN fell 500 ft to his DEATH FROM turkey PEN PEAK in YELLOW STONE PARK.
HE WAS SEARCHING FOR THE 'FENN TREASURE'.

F.F.

FORREST FENN ALLEGEDLY HID A MILLION DOLLAR TREASURE IN THE ROCKY MOUNTAINS.

BISON vs BUFFALO

BISON	BUFFALO
• LIVES IN NORTH AMERICA	• LIVES IN ASIA + AFRICA
• BIG BACK HUMP	• LITTLE BACK HUMP
• LARGE BODY	• LARGE HORNS
• NAME IS GREEK FOR 'BEEF ANIMAL'	• NAME IS FRENCH FOR 'BEEF ANIMAL'

40

Wilcoxson iCE CREAM iS THE OLDEST SUPPLiER OF GOODS to YELLOW-STONE PARK.

WiLCOXSON

iCE

CREAM

est. 1912 LIVING-STON, MONTANA

41

IN 1907 AN OBNOXIOUS ENTREPRENEUR NAMED E.C. WATERS ABANDONED his NAMESAKE STEAMSHIP ON yellowstone LAKE BECAUSE YELLOWSTONE PARK officials REFUSED to LICENSE IT AS A FERRY.

43

CHRISTMAS IN AUGUST*
is AN ANNUAL TRADITION IN YELLOWSTONE PARK the CELEBRATION INCLUDES:

GIFT GIVING   CAROLING   TREE DECORATION

* FORMELY 'SAVAGE XMAS'

44

45

THE MUMMY CAVE NEAR Yellowstone PARK IS A ROCK SHELTER WHERE A 1000 YEAR OLD MUMMY WAS FOUND.

"MUMMY JOE" WAS FOUND buried BENEATH A CAIRN.

ANCIENT tools SOURCED @OBSIDIAN CLIFF IN yellowSTONE PARK HAVE BEEN FOUND AS FAR AWAY AS MAINE.

the BEAR LUNCH COUNTER

FROM **1890** to **WWII**
YELLOWSTONE **PARK** OFFICIALS
PROVIDED **AN OPEN** TRASH
DUMP to **ATTRACT** BEARS
for TOURISTS TO
VIEW.

the 'OYSTER HOT SPRING' IN YELLOWSTONE PARK was RENAMED 'BELGIUM POOL' AFTER A VISITOR FROM belgium FATALLY fell INTO iT.

1929

49

YOU CAN see YOUR SHADOW FROM STARLIGHT ON A MOONLESS NIGHT IN yellowSTONE PARK.

50

A NASA solution TO PREVENT A YELLOWSTONE SUPERVOLCANO ERUPTION iS TO COOL iTS MAGMA WiTH WATER.

51

in 2016 MORE THAN 4000 FiSH DiED IN the YELLOWSTONE river FROM A PARASITE WHOSE CLOSEST ANIMAL RELATIVE iS A JELLYFiSH.

AN UNKNOWN NUMBER OF DUD artillery ROUNDS LITTER the SLOPES ABOVE SYLVAN PASS in YELLOWSTONE park. these UNDETONATED SHELLS ARE FROM A CANNON USED to BLAST SNOW AND MITIGATE AVALANCHE RISKS.

the WORLD'S TALLEST GEYSER:

UP TO 380 FEET

IS THE steamboat GEYSER **IN** YELLOW- STONE PARK.

GEYSER is FROM the ICELANDIC VERB **geysa** MEANING: 'to GUSH'

MORE THAN 1/2 OF THE WORLD'S GEYSERS ARE IN YELLOWSTONE.

the **BOILING** RIVER is a NATURAL HOT tub in YELLOWSTONE PARK'S GARDNER RIVER.

YELLOWSTONE PARK HAS 1000 to 3000 EARTHQUAKES PER YEAR.

56

GAS from NORRIS BASIN IN yellowSTONE PARK KILLED 5 BISON AT ONCE IN 2004.

Since THE 1995 RE-INTRODUCTION OF WOLVES into YELLOWSTONE PARK, DIMINISHED ASPEN tree POPULATIONS HAVE recovered.

58

PARKITECTURE is a STYLE OF ARChiTECTURE FOR CREATING buildings THAT HARMONIZE w/ their NATURAL SURROUNDINGS.

(TRAILSIDE MUSEUM YELLOWSTONE PARK)

59

WANDERING GARTER snake is the MOST COMMON REPTILE in YELLOWSTONE PARK.

NOT POISONOUS BUT has toxic SALIVA.

GIVES OFF FOUL ODOR FOR DEFENSE

60

BATH lake IN YELLOWSTONE PARK WAS TEMPORARILY CLOSED IN 1886 because OF TROUBLESOME MALE NUDITY.

DRIED UP IN 1984

LIGHTNING has STRUCK visitors in the SAME AREA in 2005 (11 INJURED) AND 2011 (9 INJURED) WHILE THEY WAITED FOR OLD FAITHFUL TO ERUPT.

YELLOWSTONE is A 1985 STRATEGY BOARD GAME WHERE the PLAYER w/ the MOST HERD ANIMALS @ the END OF WINTER WINS.

BOOK

GAME BOX

YELLOWSTONE

GAME BOARD

SCORE CARD

GAME PIECES

YELLOWSTONE PARK'S HART LAKE WAS NAMED AFTER HART HUNNEY IN 1840 AND RENAMED HEART LAKE after A SURVEYOR OBSERVED ITS HEART SHAPE.
I DON'T SEE IT.

AT ONE time, iN YELLOWSTONE, THERE were 60+ PLACE NAMES w/ THE word DEViL iN THEM.

A time CAPSULE WITHIN yellowSTONE PARK'S ROOSEVELT ARCH CONTAINS:

A BIBLE

A PIC OF THE U.S. PRESIDENT

COINS

MASONIC DOCUMENTS

NEWSPAPERS

IN 2015 AN AERIAL DRONE CRASHED into YELLOWSTONE'S 3RD LARGEST HOT SPRING. ITS PILOT WAS FINED $3200 + BANNED from the PARK.
WE STILL CAN'T FIND IT.

THOMAS MORAN'S PAINTING 'the GRAND CANYON OF the YELLOWSTONE' IN 1872 SERVED as INSPIRATION for the INITIAL CONSERVATION OF YELLOWSTONE PARK.

THOROFARE PATROL CABIN (in) YELLOWSTONE national **PARK** is THE MOST REMOTE DWELLING (in) the LOWER 48 STATES. it IS MORE THAN 30 MILES from THE NEAREST ROAD.

THE DEVIL'S  KITCHEN

IS A CAVERN IN yellowsTONE PARK THAT tourists DESCEND INTO BY LADDER THROUGH AN 8FT HOLE. the ATTRACTION WAS CLOSED in 1939 DUE TO HIGH CARBON DIOXIDE LEVELS.

IN A FACILITY NEAR YELLOWSTONE PARK

COMPANIES HAVE THEIR PRODUCTS TESTED BY BEARS to PREVENT HUMAN/BEAR CONFLICT.

71

SMITH MANSION

is A RUSTIC, PSYCHE-
DELIC 5-STORY
STRUCTURE NEAR
YELLOWSTONE PARK.
iTS architect
DIED WHILE
BUILDING iT.

72

YOGI IS A ROBOT USED TO EXPLORE the FLOOR OF YELLOWSTONE LAKE. OVER $100,000 IN KICKSTARTER PLEDGES FUNDED M M :* his CREATION.

NATIVE AMERICANS HAVE lived in YELLOWSTONE FOR 11,000 years.

74

FAMOUS YELLOWSTONE PARK STAFFERS

FORMER U.S. PRESIDENT LYNDON B. JOHNSON

WAS A RANGER

ACADEMY AWARD WINNING ACTOR GARY COOPER

WAS A BUS DRIVER

YELLOWSTONE PARK is the US's 1ST NATIONAL PARK.

PRESIDENT GRANT established THE PARK in 1872.

76

CINNABAR WAS the (1ST) YELLOWSTONE PARK (GATEWAY TOWN).

BUT (IN) 1903 the TRAIN STATION CLOSED AND the TOWN (WAS) ABANDONED.

HOT SPRINGS

ARE GEOTHERMAL SPRINGS PRODUCED BY HEATED GROUNDWATER THAT RISES FROM THE EARTH'S CRUST.

78

YELLOWSTONE PARK RELEASES 60 tons OF HELIUM PER YEAR THROUGH STEAM VENTS which is ENOUGH to FILL 55 GOODYEAR BLIMPS. ..

79

A MUDPOT (OR MUD POOL) is liquid DECOMPOSED ROCK in an ACIDIC HOT SPRING with limited WATER.

SMELLS LIKE ROTTEN EGGS.

80

7 FT TALL

400 POUNDS

YELLOWSTONE (PARK's) 'BEAR 399' IS the MOST FAMOUS GRIZZLY bear MOTHER in the WORLD. SHE IS 24 YEARS OLD (ANCIENT IN BEAR YEARS), HAS 40+ PHOTO-GRAPHERS AND MULTIPLE SOCIAL MEDIA ACCOUNTS W/ 1000s OF FOLLOWERS.

81

A PROTEIN taken FROM BACTERIA THRIVING in YELLOWSTONE PARK'S HOT SPRINGS IS A KEY COMPONENT ALLOWING SCIENTISTS to TEST FOR CORONAVIRUS IN SAMPLES FROM COVID-19 PATIENTS.

82

the ONLY KNOWN lizard in YELLOWSTONE PARK is the SAGEBRUSH LIZARD

they ARE 5" LONG, SKITTISH + CAN BE FOUND near HOT SPRINGS.

YELLOWSTONE PARK'S SO-CALLED ZONE of DEATH IS A 50 SQUARE MILE AREA WHERE (ACCORDING TO A LEGAL SCHOLAR) CRIME CAN be COMMITTED WITHOUT PROSECUTION.

ONLY 2 plants IN YELLOWSTONE PARK ARE POISONOUS ENOUGH to KILL A HUMAN.

water HEMLOCK
- COUSIN KILLED SOCRATES
- MISTAKEN FOR PARSNIPS

death CAMAS
- MADE SOME MEMBERS OF LEWIS + CLARK PARTY SICK
- BULB MISTAKEN FOR ONIONS

86

YellowSTONE PARK'S PETRIFIED FORESTS HAVE UPRIGHT stone TREES. THEIR ROOTS STILL REMAIN AS THEY were MILLIONS OF years AGO.

SAGEBRUSH

(A SHRUB COMMONLY FOUND IN YELLOWSTONE PARK) CAN live UP TO 200 YEARS OLD.

88

the **MAMMOTH HOTEL** in YELLOWSTONE PARK HAS AN 8FT×10FT HANDMADE MAP OF THE U.S. W/ 2500 inlaid WOOD PIECES. ONE OF ITS ARTISANS MADE BALTIMORE the CAPITAL OF MARYLAND BY MISTAKE.

MARYLAND'S ACTUAL CAPITAL IS ANNAPOLIS.

YELLOWSTONE PARK IS THE ONLY PLACE IN THE U.S. THAT BISON HAVE LIVED CONTINUOUSLY SINCE PREHISTORIC TIMES.

NAMED (AFTER) COLORFUL CLOWNS FROM EUROPE, (HARLEQUIN DUCKS) FOUND IN YELLOWSTONE PARK ARE ALSO CALLED:

LORDS + LADIES

SEA MICE

SQUEAKERS

92

SOME yellowstone WOLF FACTS

HEAVIEST KNOWN WOLF: 148 LBS.

FASTEST SPEED 35 MPH

SMELL 1000x BETTER THAN HUMANS

MATING SYSTEM IS MONOGAMOUS

ELK KILLED/YEAR PER WOLF: 18-22

OF TEETH IN ADULTS: 42
HUMANS HAVE 32

though BEAR SPRAY is 90% EFFECTiVE iN COUNTERiNG BEAR ATTACKS ONLY 28% OF YELLOWSTONE BACKCOUNTRY HiKERS carry BEAR SPRAY.*

*FROM A RECENT SURVEY

94

YELLOWTONE CAMPERS 1945-90 WERE WELL BUILT AND the TRAILER OF choice FOR CARNIVAL EMPLOYEES. "GOOD ON THE GO AND GREAT WHEN YOU GET THERE."

95

FOR 32 YEARS the US ARMY MANAGED YELLOWSTONE PARK BEFORE TRANSFERRING IT to THE NATIONAL PARK SERVICE in 1918.

CAPTAIN MOSES HARRIS WAS THE 1ST PARK SUPER-INTENDENT

96

LAKE MUSIC is A MYSTERY SOUND THAT CAN BE HEARD ON YELLOW-STONE lake.

BUNSEN PEAK in YELLOWSTONE PARK is a 8,564 FT tall INTRUSION OF MAGMA NAMED AFTER ROBERT BUNSEN (PHYSICIST) WHO RE-SEARCHED GEYSERS & helped INVENT THE BUNSEN BURNER

YARNS OF the YELLOW-STONE

IS AN ANECDOTAL, HISTORICAL COMIC BOOK ABOUT life IN YELLOWSTONE PARK. it WAS WRITTEN, DRAWN + PUBLISHED IN 1972 by BILL CHAPMAN: ARTIST, PILOT, WRANGLER + SON OF A RANGER.

NATIVE AMERICAN ✿ NAMES

for THE YELLOWSTONE PARK AREA

TRIBE	TRANSLATED WORD	
SIOUX	WHITE MOUNTAIN COUNTRY	
BLACK-FOOT	MANY SMOKE	
NEZ PERCE	LAND OF STREAM	
SHOSHONE	UP HIGH	

100

THE 1959 YELLOWSTONE earthquake WAS SO POWERFUL, it DESTROYED A MOUNTAIN + MADE A LAKE.

85000 TON SLIDE

NEW LAKE

THANKS TO MY WiFE tricia.

iF YOU like THiS BOOK TRY **MONTANA** QUiCK **FACTS**, AVAiLABLE AT THE COOLEST BOOK SHOPS OR ONLINE.

CPSIA information can be obtained
at www.ICGtesting.com
Printed in the USA
LVHW071521230622
721976LV00007B/183